W9-AYV-305

THOUSANDS

BILLIONS

THOUSANDS

FACT

THOUSANDS BILLIONS

FICTION

KEN HAM

illustrated by

BILL LOONEY

DINOSAURS
for kids

DEDICATION:

This book which represents the Godly Heritage of the Ham family is dedicated to our grandchildren:

Malachi	Kylie	Josiah
Kathryn	Caleb	Amelia
Noah	Lacey	Tiberius
Madelyn	Lexie	Declan
Emma	Nicole	Lillianne
Olivia	Kendra	Baby Ham (#18)

First printing: October 2009
Sixteenth printing: April 2022

Copyright © 2009 by Ken Ham. All rights reserved. No part of this book may be reproduced, copied, broadcast, stored, or shared in any form whatsoever without written permission from the publisher, except in the case of brief quotations in articles and reviews. For information write to:

Master Books®, P.O. Box 726, Green Forest, AR 72638

Master Books® is a division of New Leaf Publishing Group, Inc.

Please visit our web site for other great titles:
www.masterbooks.com

ISBN: 978-0-89051-555-6
ISBN: 978-1-61458-168-0 (digital)

Library of Congress Number: 2009936441

All scripture quotations are taken from the New King James Version

Illustrations by Bill Looney
Cover & Interior design by Diana Bogardus

For information regarding author interviews, please contact the publicity department at (870) 438-5288.

 « ANATOTITAN (meaning "large duck") is a duck-billed hadrosaur. It could grow to around 40 feet in length, and fed on vegetation. Paleontologists struggled to properly classify this dinosaur through the early to mid-20th century into a proper genus.

Dinosaurs can provide a great way to learn about history. You may already be familiar with some of these dinosaurs. These drawings show you what we think they may have looked like. Now, we don't know for sure, of course, as we usually only find their bones as fossils (and most times, only a few of their bones). Artists use what bones have been found, knowledge about living animals, and some imagination to come up with drawings like these. See if you can pronounce these dinosaur names:

Dilophosaurus (die-LOF-o-SAWR-us), meaning "two-crested lizard."

Styracosaurus (sty-RAK-o-SAWR-us), meaning "spiked lizard."

Triceratops (tri-SER-a-tops), meaning "three-horned face."

Megalosaurus (MEG-a-lo-SAWR-us), meaning "big lizard."

MEGALOSAURUS »

Iguanodon (i-GWAHN-o-don), meaning "iguana tooth."

Ceratosaurus (ser-ah-toe-SAWR-us), meaning "horned lizard."

Deinonychus (die-NON-i-kus), meaning "terrible claws."

DEINONYCHUS »

Velociraptor (vee-LOHS-i-RAP-tor), meaning "swift robber."

Ultrasaurus (UHL-tra-SAWR-us), was so nicknamed because of its enormous size.

Seismosaurus (SIES-mo-SAWR-us), meaning "earthquake lizard."

Did you know there are hundreds of dinosaur names? However, there were not hundreds of types of dinosaurs. There were a number of similar ones that should be grouped in categories known by what the Bible describes as "kinds." Does that sound a little confusing? Well, this book will help to explain this and a lot of other things about dinosaurs you may not know.

« DILOPHOSAURUS

STYRACOSAURUS »

« TRICERATOPS

IGUANODON »

CERATOSAURUS »

« VELOCIRAPTOR

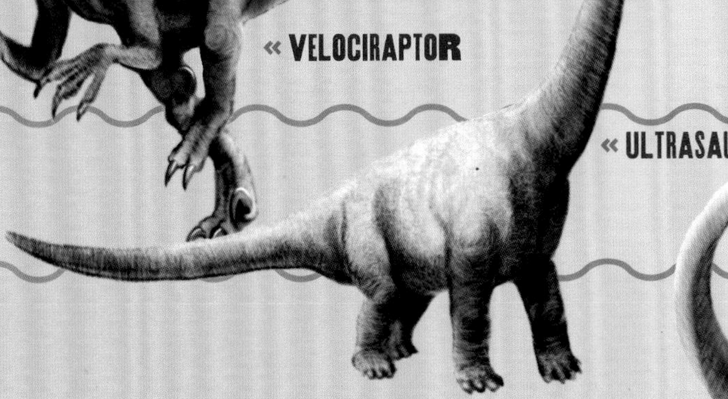

« ULTRASAURUS

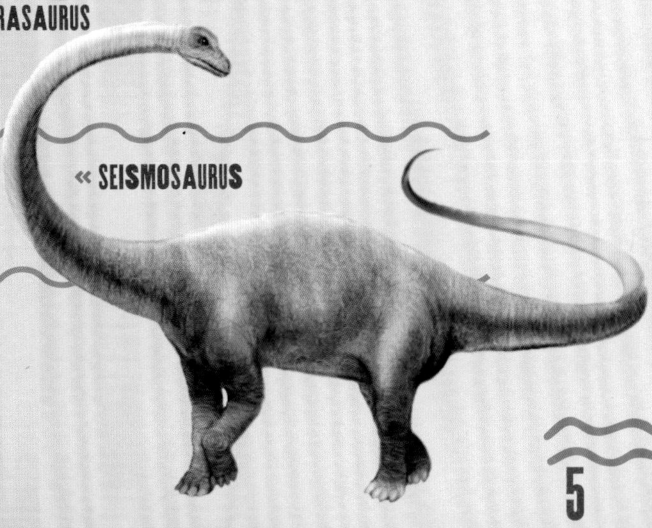

« SEISMOSAURUS

Before we begin, I don't want you to miss out on knowing what my very favorite dinosaur is! In fact, I think he deserves this whole page to himself! It is the mighty Tyrannosaurus rex (ti-RAN-oh-SAWR-us-rex), meaning "tyrant lizard king." I'll let you in on a secret—I love T-rex because I like his teeth! I use teeth to teach kids and parents some very interesting things about dinosaurs—things that you may not have heard or really understood before. But it is very important to understand the truth about dinosaurs!

FOUR
>>>> FAST FACTS

1. T-rex fossils are found in Canada and the western United States.
2. The first documented T-rex fossil was discovered in 1902 by Barnum Brown.
3. Scientists think T-rex skeletons were made up of close to 200 bones.
4. T-rex had around 60 teeth, which ranged in size based on their placement in the jaw of the skull.

T-REX »

With a strong tail extended for balance, an adult T-rex could be a little over 40 feet in length, 12 to13 feet tall at the hips, and weigh between 5 and 7 tons. T-rex's jagged teeth could be up to 9 inches long, and like sharks, the T-rex was able to replace teeth when one was lost.

What's in a name? Remember that the T-rex name means "tyrant lizard king." But secular scientists are still wondering whether T-rexes were active hunters or clever scavengers, or a combination of both. However, creation scientists are able to explain the evidence in a different way using the biblical account of history, as we will soon learn.

1. The word "fossil" is from the Latin word meaning "dug up."
2. Scientists often make assumptions about dinosaurs based on a few fossilized bones, bone fragments, or other fossil remains, impressions, etc.
3. Only a few thousand dinosaur fossil skeletons have been discovered.
4. The vast majority of fossils discovered are marine invertebrates (creatures that don't have backbones like clams).

I'm sure you have lots of questions about dinosaurs. I believe I can answer many of those questions for you because dinosaurs are not a mystery at all. I know someone who was there when dinosaurs came into existence, and was also there when they seemed to disappear from the earth. In fact, this "someone" has written a book for us that gives a detailed account of the history of the universe. He tells us when the earth began, as well as when all the living creatures and the first humans appeared.

Now, you may be asking "Who is this someone you say was there to see the dinosaurs?" He is the Creator of all things. He knows everything because He is all powerful and has always been around. And this Creator had a book written for us to give us the details of how time began, and how the universe and all life came into existence. This book also tells us who we are, where we came from, and why we exist. It also gives us information on what is going to happen in the future! There is no other book like this on earth. It is unique, and it is called…the Bible.

When you understand the Bible, you will understand more about dinosaurs. The Bible helps us to answer questions about dinosaurs and about the world around us today.

BIGGER Among the most widely known type of dinosaurs, the sauropods ("lizard foot") are some of the largest creatures to ever walk the earth. Many of these dinosaurs are known by only a few pieces of bone fragments, and debate continues on just which dinosaur was the largest ever. As discoveries continue, more will be known about these massive giants. Sauroposeidon ("earthquake god lizard") was considered the largest dinosaur ever to live, until the discovery of Argentinosaurus ("silver lizard"). Though only a few bones of each creature have been found, many scientists estimate that Argentinosaurus was larger, though Sauroposeidon may have been taller.

« SAUROPOSEIDON

« COMPSOGNATHUS

SMALLER Compsognathus ("elegant jaw") is among the smallest dinosaurs discovered. A little bigger than a chicken, this dinosaur weighed around 6 pounds. Some scientists have found smaller creatures, like Microraptors, which they try to use to prove dinosaurs were the evolutionary ancestor of birds—real science and the Bible disprove this idea. Archaeopteryx ("ancient wing") is another example of a creature once thought to prove this link, but that idea has now been proven false.

Did you know that the Bible is really a collection of books written by people specially inspired by God the Creator to write down exactly what God wanted us to know? The Bible tells us more about who God is and why we can always trust Him to tell us the truth:

1. The God of the Bible is the true God: *"But the LORD [is] the true God; He is the living God and the everlasting King…"* (Jeremiah 10:10).

2. The God of the Bible is infinite—He is all knowing, all powerful: *"Great is our Lord, and mighty in power; His understanding is infinite"* (Psalm 147:5).

3. The God of the Bible lives forever—He lives in eternity—He had no beginning and has no end: *"Now to the King eternal, immortal, invisible, to God who alone is wise, be honor and glory forever and ever…"* (I Timothy 1:17).

4. The God of the Bible is the only true God—other gods people claim to have are false gods: *"Therefore You are great, O LORD GOD. For there is none like You, nor is there any God besides…"* (2 Samuel 7:22).

5. The God of the Bible is all wise and all knowing: *"…in whom are hidden all the treasures of wisdom and knowledge."* (Colossians 2:3).

WOW!

What an awesome God.

PTEROSAUR »

« STEGOSAURUS

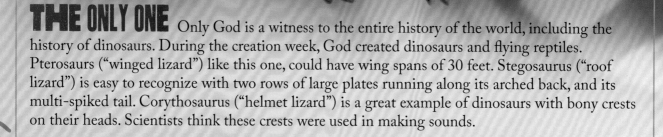

THE ONLY ONE Only God is a witness to the entire history of the world, including the history of dinosaurs. During the creation week, God created dinosaurs and flying reptiles. Pterosaurs ("winged lizard") like this one, could have wing spans of 30 feet. Stegosaurus ("roof lizard") is easy to recognize with two rows of large plates running along its arched back, and its multi-spiked tail. Corythosaurus ("helmet lizard") is a great example of dinosaurs with bony crests on their heads. Scientists think these crests were used in making sounds.

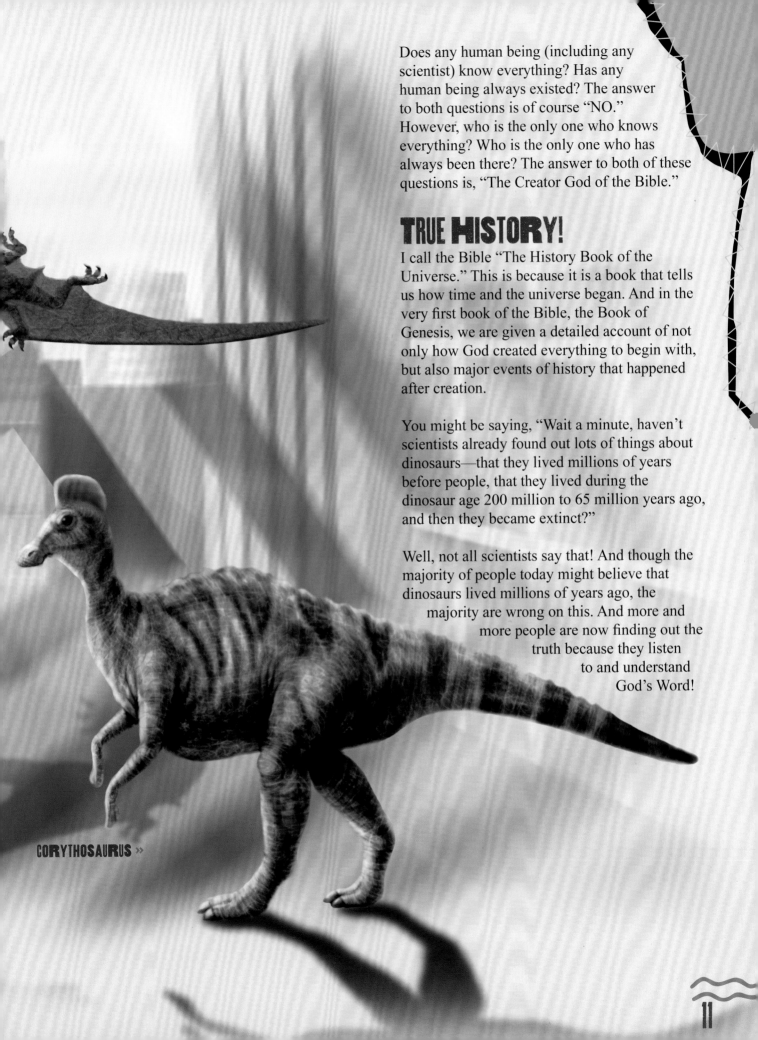

Does any human being (including any scientist) know everything? Has any human being always existed? The answer to both questions is of course "NO." However, who is the only one who knows everything? Who is the only one who has always been there? The answer to both of these questions is, "The Creator God of the Bible."

TRUE HISTORY!

I call the Bible "The History Book of the Universe." This is because it is a book that tells us how time and the universe began. And in the very first book of the Bible, the Book of Genesis, we are given a detailed account of not only how God created everything to begin with, but also major events of history that happened after creation.

You might be saying, "Wait a minute, haven't scientists already found out lots of things about dinosaurs—that they lived millions of years before people, that they lived during the dinosaur age 200 million to 65 million years ago, and then they became extinct?"

Well, not all scientists say that! And though the majority of people today might believe that dinosaurs lived millions of years ago, the majority are wrong on this. And more and more people are now finding out the truth because they listen to and understand God's Word!

CORYTHOSAURUS »

On the basis of the Bible's history, and what we observe in today's world, I have outlined seven "ages" that apply to dinosaurs. Each age represents an important period in what we know about dinosaurs. Let me list them for you, and then we will learn more about each one in the following sections:

AGE ONE: FORMED – the age when all animals were created

AGE TWO: FEARLESS – the age when all animals and people lived together without fear

AGE THREE: FALLEN – the age when sin came and dinosaurs started to die

AGE FOUR: FLOOD – the age when most dinosaur fossils were formed

AGE FIVE: FADED – the age when dinosaurs died out and became extinct

AGE SIX: FOUND – the age when evidence of dinosaurs was rediscovered

AGE SEVEN: FICTION – the age we live in, when untrue stories about dinosaurs and millions of years are taught through books, television, and schools

MIXING FACT WITH FICTION

When you visit most museums that feature dinosaur collections, you will see a mix of fact and fiction. Some scientists draw conclusions and make assumptions about the lives of dinosaurs based on very little actual evidence. They then present that as truth in very detailed multimedia displays.

THOUSANDS BILLIONS

TYRANNOSAURUS REX AND STEGOSAURUS

1. Museums add to their collections through expeditions, donated specimens, public auctions of fossils, and private purchases.
2. Large dinosaur fossil finds are rare and are often sold for hundreds of thousands of dollars each.
3. The Chicago Field Museum spent a record $8 million for a nearly-complete T-rex nicknamed "Sue."
4. Millions of fossils have been found and classified; only a tiny fraction are placed on display.

Did you know you can ask very simple questions to the scientists who claim that dinosaurs lived millions of years ago? You could say to them, in a very nice way of course, "Excuse me, were you there?" You are actually asking them, "Were you there to see the dinosaurs when they first came into existence? Were you there to see them alive? Were you there to see them die out?" Obviously, they weren't there, so how could they really know everything about them?

Today, scientists only know about dinosaurs from the fossilized bones they find. But when they dig up these bones, the fossils don't have labels on them telling how old they are. And they don't have photographs with them showing the so-called dinosaur age from 200 to 65 million years ago. These scientists have to make guesses about what happened in the past because they weren't there and don't know everything. Even things they think they know often change based on new information and discoveries.

If you take God's word in the Bible and listen to the account of history from the One who knows everything and has always been there, you can learn the truth about dinosaurs. And I also want to show you that real scientific evidence confirms the truth of the Bible's account of history. I (and many scientists I know) do not believe in the so-called "age of dinosaurs." And we certainly don't believe dinosaurs lived millions of years ago. In fact, and this may surprise you, we consider there to be SEVEN ages of dinosaurs reflected in biblical history! Each one begins with the letter "F" to make them easier for you to remember.

So buckle up your seat belts as we travel back in history and solve the mystery of the dinosaurs!

FOSSIL FIND Carnotaurus ("flesh bull") is among the most bizarre dinosaurs ever discovered. This large dinosaur had two skull bones above its eyes that resembled horns. With extremely tiny arms, just four fingers, and a very long neck, this unique dinosaur's bones have been found in South America.

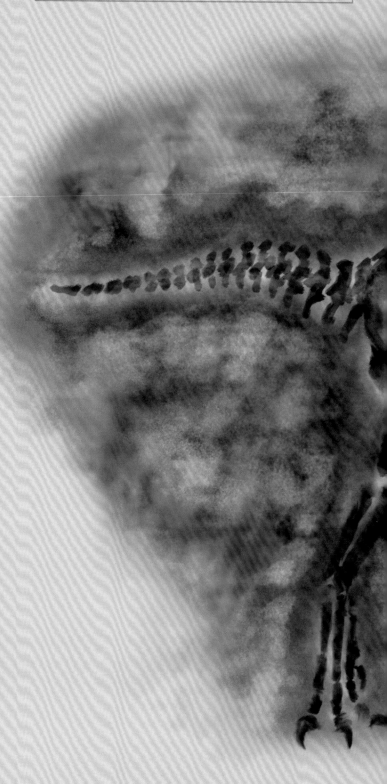

I am sure you have a lot of questions about dinosaurs:

When did they exist?

Where did they come from?

What happened to them?

Why do we find fossils of their bones all over the earth?

Why are they such a mystery?

What was the smallest dinosaur?

What was the largest dinosaur?

The 7 F's of dinosaur history answer these questions and more! Let's begin our journey of discovery at the point when and where dinosaurs began.

FOUR
>>>> FAST FACTS

1. Laws restricting or allowing fossil hunting vary by state.
2. Depending on where you find your fossil—on private or public land—there may be questions of ownership.
3. Most fossils are found in rock made of mud or sand.
4. Fossils have been discovered around the world in almost every kind of terrain.

17

AGE 1: FORMED

TWO FEET OR FOUR Massospondylus ("longer vertebrae") hatchlings; this type of dinosaur was among the first to be formally named. The first fossil of Massospondylus was found in 1854 in South America. Scientists originally thought this dinosaur walked on four legs, but recent studies point to the creature being bipedal (walking on its hind legs). There are reports that fossil egg nests have been discovered, though not all scientists agree that dinosaurs formed nests.

When the King James Bible was first translated into English in 1611, the word "dinosaur" did not exist. The word dinosaur was invented in 1841 by an English scientist named Sir Richard Owen. It was created for a particular group of land animals and it is still the word we use to describe these creatures today.

GOD CREATED

Now that we know how they got the name dinosaur, let's discover how they came into existence. Some want to say that the dinosaurs took millions of years to evolve and appear, but this isn't real history. In the Bible. God gives us a true account of when He made all the land animals:

Then God said, "Let the earth bring forth the living creature according to its kind: cattle and creeping thing and beast of the earth, each according to its kind"; and it was so. And God made the beast of the earth according to its kind, cattle according to its kind, and everything that creeps on the earth according to its kind. And God saw that it was good… (Genesis1:24, 25).

Because dinosaurs were land animals, this means every kind of dinosaur (including the T-rex kind) was made on day six of the creation week. God made them like He made all other animals on the earth.

SIXTH DAY

Just wait until you read the next event that occurred on the sixth day of creation as recorded in Genesis 1:26, 27:

Then God said, "Let Us make man in Our image, according to Our likeness…So God created man in His own image; in the image of God He created him; male and female He created them.

This means that each kind of dinosaur (including my favorite—the T-rex kind) was created on the same day that God made the first two people, Adam and Eve! Do you realize what that means? It means dinosaurs and people lived together.

Because land animals were made before the first man and woman, if anyone tells you that dinosaurs existed before people, you can say, "they sure did—they existed probably just a few hours before people!" That should create some interesting conversations for you!

SIX REAL DAYS Have you ever wondered why we have a seven-day week? Why not a ten-day week or a five-day week? There is only one reason we have a seven-day week, and it comes from the Bible. God created everything in six days, and rested for one, setting a pattern for us. That's why we have a seven-day week!

Now, if God created everything over millions of years, as some people try to say, then the seven-day week would not make sense. For instance, if God made everything in six million years and then rested for one million years, then our week would be millions and millions of years long! It is very obvious from the language in the Book of Genesis, and what God explains about the seven-day week, that God created everything in six literal days (approximately 24 hours each), and rested for one literal day, an example which serves as a basis for the seven-day week. Information from the Bible and other sources allow us to add up dates to find out that God created the universe about 6,000 years ago!

EVOLUTIONARY BELIEF <<<<<

HOW DID LIFE BEGIN? In order to properly understand both science and history, you need to start at the beginning. Knowing how and when life began is key to understanding not only dinosaurs, but also the world we live in today. There are two primary explanations to answer the question of how life began:

1. The belief in evolution based on the idea that life arose by itself without any intelligence involved.
2. The creation account as recorded in the Bible in the Book of Genesis—that the infinite Creator God created all things just as recorded.

3.0 BYA Rocks from this time are metamorphic or igneous, showing changing conditions. The first supercontinents begin to form.

3.5 BYA Bacteria now appear and the fossil record begins.

2.5 BYA Traces of oxygen appear, and supercontinents begin breaking apart.

>>>> FICTION

4.0 BYA The moon formed from a damaging space collision with earth and its magnetic forces. Oceans may have been formed a few 100 million years after this point.

2.0 BYA Single cells with a nucleus evolved.

4.5 BYA The earth forms around 4.5 billion years ago.

MYA = million years ago
BYA = billion years ago

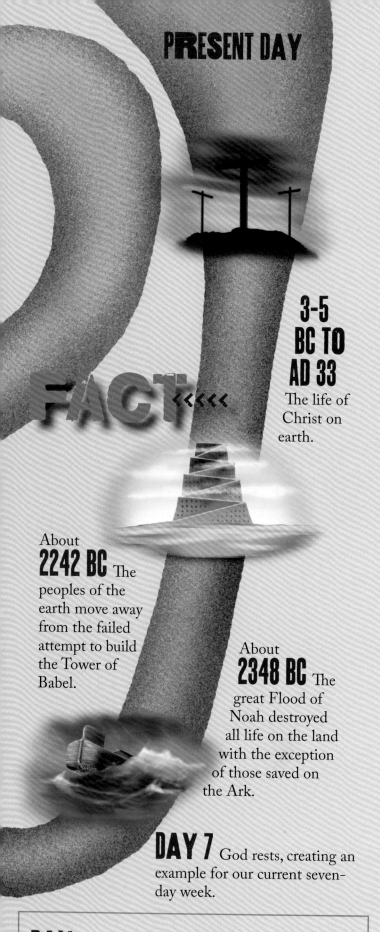

FACT <<<<

3-5 BC TO AD 33 The life of Christ on earth.

About **2242 BC** The peoples of the earth move away from the failed attempt to build the Tower of Babel.

About **2348 BC** The great Flood of Noah destroyed all life on the land with the exception of those saved on the Ark.

DAY 7 God rests, creating an example for our current seven-day week.

DAY = literal 24-hours
BC = Before Christ
AD = After Christ's birth

BIBLICAL TRUTH

ADDING IT UP Have you ever seen passages in the Bible like this one:

"And Adam lived one hundred and thirty years, and begot a son in his own likeness, after his image, and named him Seth. After he begot Seth, the days of Adam were eight hundred years; and he had sons and daughters. So all the days that Adam lived were nine hundred and thirty years; and he died. Seth lived one hundred and five years, and begot Enosh. After he begot Enosh, Seth lived eight hundred and seven years, and had sons and daughters. So all the days of Seth were nine hundred and twelve years; and he died. Enosh lived ninety years, and begot Cainan. After he begot Cainan, Enosh lived eight hundred and fifteen years, and had sons and daughters..." (Genesis 5:5-10).

Passages like this tell us when people were born and died down through the ages. There are many more like this that help us to add up dates to find out that God began creating the universe on the first day of the creation week, about 6,000 years ago!

So we could say that the first dinosaur age began about 6,000 years ago! And if someone says, "No, it was millions of years ago," remember the question you nicely ask them: "Excuse me, but were you there?" And if they answer, "No, I wasn't there, but you weren't either," do you know what you should then say? I suggest you say, "No I wasn't there, but I know Someone who was, and I have His Word. Are you interested to hear what He has to say?"

THOUSANDS BILLIONS <<<<

23

EUDIMORPHODON »

RHAMPHORHYNCHUS »

« PTERODACTYL

QUETZALCOATLUS »

PASSING TIME Genealogies (family histories) in the Bible give us important and thorough chronological evidence. Chronology is the scientific study of dates to determine the time of certain historical events.

FLYING REPTILES

EUDIMORPHODON had teeth that changed as the creature got older. It could have over a hundred teeth in a 2.5 inch jaw, some of which had multiple points. It also had longer fang-like teeth at the front.

DIMORPHODON wasn't among the largest pterosaurs, with a wing span of less than five feet. However, it did have a short neck and an unusually-shaped head, with wide jaws and a deep skull. A flap of skin on the end of its thin tail helped it to fly better.

RHAMPHORHYNCHUS had a tail feature similar to Dimorphodon, but its teeth were shaped more like needles and pointed forward, though at the front of the jaw, there were no teeth.

PTERODACTYL was the first of the flying reptiles to be named and classified, though long after its discovery in the 1780s. Like other pterosaurs, they had wings made of skin and muscle stretching from their long fingers to their legs. Fossils of this flying reptile show a wing span of a foot and a half, with a crest on its head, sheathed claws, and a mane on its neck.

PTERODAUSTRO featured a jaw with a dense set of bristle-like teeth. With its jaw curving upward, it is thought this creature sifted its food by dipping its jaws into the water like a basket or a net.

QUETZALCOATLUS is named after an ancient Aztec god. Originally discovered in Texas, the fossil of this flying reptile had a massive wing span of over 32 feet. Because of the shape and size of its body, it is thought these creatures walked on all fours, but that is just an idea scientists have. With little fossil evidence, scientists are still trying to determine just how much this majestic creature even weighed.

« DIMORPHODON

« PTERODAUSTRO

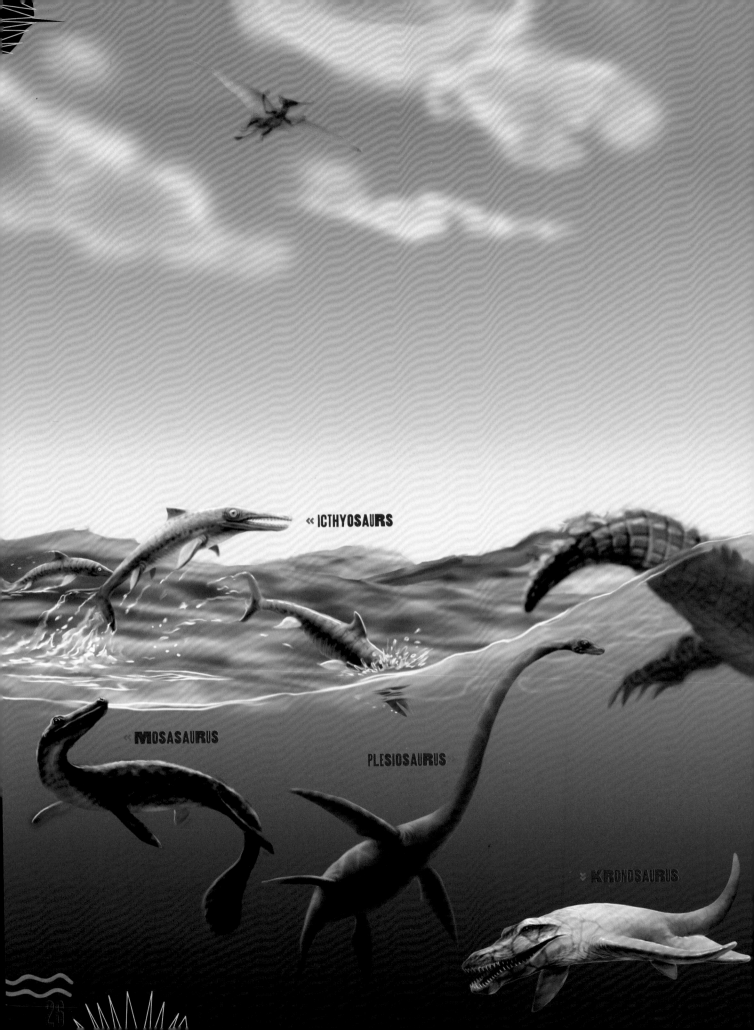

ICTHYOSAURS

MOSASAURUS

PLESIOSAURUS

KRONDSAURUS

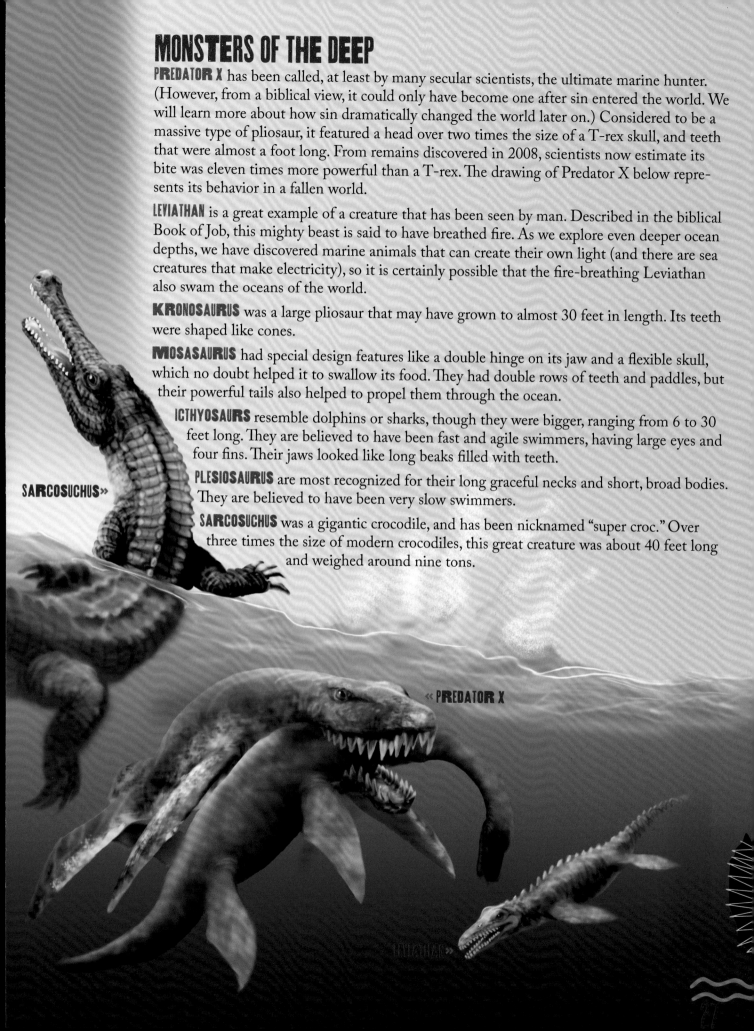

MONSTERS OF THE DEEP

PREDATOR X has been called, at least by many secular scientists, the ultimate marine hunter. (However, from a biblical view, it could only have become one after sin entered the world. We will learn more about how sin dramatically changed the world later on.) Considered to be a massive type of pliosaur, it featured a head over two times the size of a T-rex skull, and teeth that were almost a foot long. From remains discovered in 2008, scientists now estimate its bite was eleven times more powerful than a T-rex. The drawing of Predator X below represents its behavior in a fallen world.

LEVIATHAN is a great example of a creature that has been seen by man. Described in the biblical Book of Job, this mighty beast is said to have breathed fire. As we explore even deeper ocean depths, we have discovered marine animals that can create their own light (and there are sea creatures that make electricity), so it is certainly possible that the fire-breathing Leviathan also swam the oceans of the world.

KRONOSAURUS was a large pliosaur that may have grown to almost 30 feet in length. Its teeth were shaped like cones.

MOSASAURUS had special design features like a double hinge on its jaw and a flexible skull, which no doubt helped it to swallow its food. They had double rows of teeth and paddles, but their powerful tails also helped to propel them through the ocean.

ICTHYOSAURS resemble dolphins or sharks, though they were bigger, ranging from 6 to 30 feet long. They are believed to have been fast and agile swimmers, having large eyes and four fins. Their jaws looked like long beaks filled with teeth.

PLESIOSAURUS are most recognized for their long graceful necks and short, broad bodies. They are believed to have been very slow swimmers.

SARCOSUCHUS was a gigantic crocodile, and has been nicknamed "super croc." Over three times the size of modern crocodiles, this great creature was about 40 feet long and weighed around nine tons.

SARCOSUCHUS»

« PREDATOR X

LEVIATHAN»

AGE 2: FEARLESS

When God finished creating the land animals, Genesis chapter one states, *"And God saw that it was good."* And then at the end of day six, when God had finished creating everything, He said everything was *"very good."*

Now keep this in mind as we also read two more verses from Genesis 1:29, 30:

"And God said, "See, I have given you every herb that yields seed which is on the face of all the earth, and every tree whose fruit yields seed; to you it shall be for food. "Also, to every beast of the earth, to every bird of the air, and to everything that creeps on the earth, in which there is life, I have given every green herb for food"; and it was so."

Humans and animals were given fruit and plants to eat.

Try to imagine a world where everything is very good. There is no disease or sickness. Animals and humans are not afraid of each other. People don't eat animals, and animals don't eat people—they all eat plants. So often we see images of the Garden of Eden filled only with animals we see living today. But it would have had dinosaurs as well.

It's hard to imagine, isn't it, because we live in such a different world today (and we will find out why soon).

WHOSE TOOTH WAS IT?

A tooth can be a good way to identify a dinosaur, but it isn't always easy. Dinosaur teeth come in all shapes and sizes. Some types of dinosaurs had teeth that ranged from very large to very small in one animal, making it difficult to tell if a single tooth is from a large dinosaur or a smaller dinosaur of the same variety. The shape of a tooth can be more helpful for identification than size.

A general way of telling what kind of dinosaur had a particular tooth is by shape. Molars that looked like a leaf with grooves are from dinosaurs like ankylosaurs or ceratopsians. Teeth that are pointed and look like a slightly curved knife blade, that narrows to a sharp, jagged edge like a saw, are found such in dinosaurs like raptors and T-rex. Sauropod teeth were straight, more round, with a blunt top, almost like a chisel or even a spoon.

Secular scientists try to guess what dinosaurs ate by the shape of their teeth. But their guesses are often wrong. In Genesis 1:30 we find the real truth: *Also, to every beast of the earth, to every bird of the air, and to everything that creeps on the earth, in which there is life, I have given every green herb for food; and it was so.*

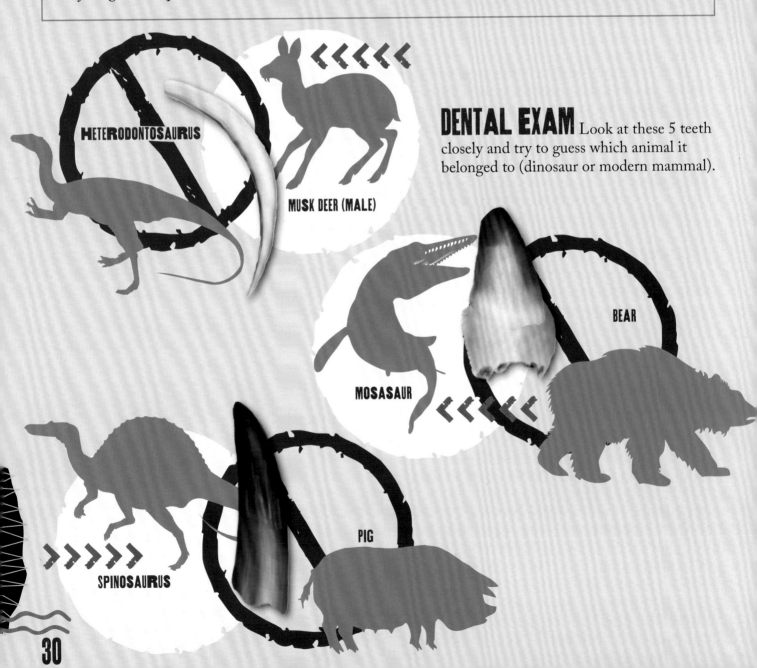

HETERODONTOSAURUS

MUSK DEER (MALE)

DENTAL EXAM Look at these 5 teeth closely and try to guess which animal it belonged to (dinosaur or modern mammal).

MOSASAUR

BEAR

SPINOSAURUS

PIG

When God finished creating everything, this was truly the Fearless age—the age when people and animals were unafraid of each other. The age when a T-rex could put his head beside Adam, open his mouth, and show all those teeth (remember, I like T-rex because of his teeth), and Adam wouldn't have been afraid! Adam knew that T-rex (as we now call him) only ate plants.

Now, I can just hear some of you saying, "But T-rex had sharp teeth, so he was obviously a meat eater." Are you really sure? Can you really assume that? Just because an animal has sharp teeth doesn't mean it is a meat eater. It just means what?… of course—it has sharp teeth!

Let's see if you can think of animals that live in today's world that have sharp, frightening-looking teeth to us, but they eat mainly plants? Let me list some:

The Australian fruit bat—what a savage looking creature! He flies around Australia and rips up and eats…fruit!

Did you know most bears are primarily vegetarian, and certain bears are almost solely vegetarian. But they have sharp looking teeth like that of a tiger. In certain circumstances, however, they can

be quite savage and kill people in the present world, but they don't attack humans to eat them.

So why did animals like T-rex need sharp teeth if they weren't eating meat? Well, if you are going to eat certain plants, branches, vegetables, and fruits (like pumpkins and watermelons), you would need very sharp teeth!

Are you thinking, "Ok, but today there are animals who eat other animals, and even people, and people eat animals—what happened?" That is the right question to ask. What happened is that an event changed everything, and led to the third age of dinosaurs—the Fallen age.

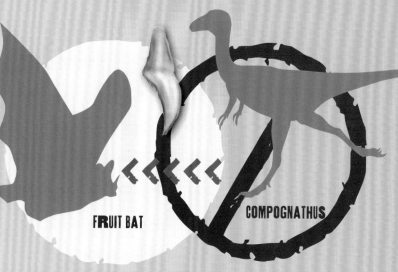

FRUIT BAT

COMPOGNATHUS

T-REX

HEDGE HOG

TOOTHY MYSTERY At only six - feet long, Troodon (whose name means "wounding tooth") wasn't the biggest dinosaur around, but it did have a very large brain in comparison to its overall size. The Troodon's body shape appears to be that of a fast runner, and with jagged teeth, it's easy to see why secular scientists originally thought it was a predator.

WHAT'S FOR DINNER?
In this fallen world (suffering the effects of sin and the curse), secular scientists often classify dinosaurs by what they think they ate. They placed dinosaurs in one of three categories by observing what the dinosaur had eaten at the time of its death, and the shape of its teeth.

OMNIVORE—eating both meat and plants

HERBIVORE—eating plants and vegetation

CARNIVORE—eating only meat

However, before the fall (before sin), all dinosaurs (regardless of the type of teeth they had), would have been classified as herbivores or vegetarians.

FOUR FAST FACTS

1. Amber is fossilized resin, not sap, from trees.
2. Amber is often used to make jewelry—and can even contain insects "frozen" in time.
3. Some scientists try to extract DNA from the blood of creatures trapped in amber in hopes of learning more.
4. Despite the premise of the movie *Jurassic Park,* most scientists say it is impossible to recreate dinosaurs from the DNA found in amber.

LIVING FOSSILS
These fossilized plants are identical to plants living today.

LIFE IN GOD'S GARDEN

What was the Garden of Eden? Here is what God's Word tells us about this incredible paradise (Genesis 2:8-17):

The LORD God planted a garden eastward in Eden, and there He put the man whom He had formed. And out of the ground the LORD God made every tree grow that is pleasant to the sight and good for food. The tree of life was also in the midst of the garden, and the tree of the knowledge of good and evil. Now a river went out of Eden to water the garden, and from there it parted and became four riverheads. The name of the first is Pishon; it is the one which skirts the whole land of Havilah, where there is gold. And the gold of that land is good. Bdellium and the onyx stone are there. The name of the second river is Gihon; it is the one which goes around the whole land of Cush. The name of the third river is Hiddekel; it is the one which goes toward the east of Assyria. The fourth river is the Euphrates.

Then the LORD God took the man and put him in the garden of Eden to tend and keep it. And the LORD God commanded the man, saying, "Of every tree of the garden you may freely eat; but of the tree of the knowledge of good and evil you shall not eat, for in the day that you eat of it you shall surely die."

SOLVING THE MYSTERY

As we have seen, God created the world and all the animals, including dinosaurs, and they lived for a time in peace without harming one another. Eating fruit and other vegetation, dinosaurs lived together with other animals and with the first humans. As we are about to see, it wasn't a change in climate or a natural disaster that brought death into this perfect world, but it was Adam and Eve's act of disobedience. This act would bring a terrible consequence to both mankind and animals. Adam and Eve chose to disobey God, and the world would never be the same.

PREY OR PLAY? Smaller dinosaurs like the swan-sized Segisaurus ("Segi canyon lizard") would have eaten vegetation or fruit in the Garden of Eden.

AGE 3: FALLEN

Let's all be very still and really quiet for a just moment.

We are about to learn about what I call "the saddest day in the history of the universe." No day has ever been as sad as this day. What happened has affected the universe and everything in it to this day! It affected dinosaurs, the dirt, the stars, people (including you and me)—it affected everything!

At some point after this day, dinosaurs began to hunt other animals to eat. The paradise where they had lived in peace became a grim world where death became a part of their life. People and animals were no longer fearless—it was becoming a violent world.

SO WHAT HAPPENED?

I have a dinosaur puppet that I put on my hand, and I can make it move in different directions, open its mouth, and do what I want it to do. When God made Adam, God didn't make him like a puppet that God forced to do whatever He wanted him to do. He gave Adam the ability to make choices.

When He created the first man and woman, God wanted them to love Him because they chose to—not because they were forced to love Him. So God gave them a test to see if they really would love Him and obey Him.

God told Adam that they could eat the fruit of any trees—except one. This tree was called "The tree of the knowledge of good and evil." God told Adam, *but of the tree of the knowledge of good and evil you shall not eat, for in the day that you eat of it you shall surely die,* (Genesis 2:17).

YOU KNOW WHAT HAPPENED? Adam
and Eve disobeyed. They failed God's test. They could eat fruit from any other tree in this beautiful garden. But they still chose to disobey and eat from the one tree that was forbidden.

SIN AND DEATH BEGINS As Adam and Eve
hid in shame having disobeyed God's command not to eat of the tree of knowledge of good and evil, paradise began to change forever. Some dinosaurs and other animals that once only ate vegetation began to prey on other creatures. Fear and death became a part of their daily life as animals struggled to survive.

This was the saddest event, and the saddest day in the history of the universe. Adam rebelled against his Creator—this is called sin. And because of sin, now we die as God warned would happen. Because Adam sinned, all people (including you and me) are sinners. And this sin separates us from God. One day our bodies will die, and our souls (the real "us" that lives in our bodies) will be separated from God forever because of sin! What a terrible situation!

But God had a plan. He knew we would be sinners—He knew Adam would eat that fruit from the forbidden tree. God had a plan to pay for our sin so that after we die, we could go to heaven to live with God forever.

JESUS IS THE ANSWER

About 2,000 years ago, God sent his Son to earth to be a perfect man (the God-man). His Son, the Lord Jesus, became a baby, born in Bethlehem. He (who was both God and man at the same time) grew up to be a man—but He was the only man to never sin. He then died on a cross to pay the penalty for our sin. He had to be perfect and without sin to be a perfect sacrifice because of our sin. He died because death was the judgment for sin, but then He was raised from the dead, thus conquering death.

The good news is that for all those humans who repent and put their faith and trust in Jesus as the One who died for them and paid for their sin, and receive Him into their life—they will live forever with Him.

I pray that you have put your faith and trust in the Lord Jesus. That is the most important thing for you to do in the entire universe! In the meantime—here's the bad news! Since the time Adam sinned, an event we refer to as "the Fall" (because Adam "fell" from a perfect state to be a sinner), the world is no longer "very good." Sin has affected everything in the universe, and it affected dinosaurs too.

We don't know when they started eating each other, but sometime after sin, certain animals started eating others. No doubt some of them would have become quite aggressive and frightening to people.

When you sin, things get worse and worse. After about 1,500 years, all the people on earth—except one family of eight—had rebelled against God!

It was so bad that God planned to bring a great judgment on the world—a judgment by water. God told Noah He was going to send a great flood that would cover the entire earth and destroy everything.

Yes, the next age of dinosaurs—the age of the Flood—was about to begin.

VIOLENCE AND DEATH

Two scavenging dinosaurs battle fiercely. This cycle of life and death began with the Fall and still is seen in our world today.

AGE 4: FLOOD

Around 4,500 years ago, God told Noah to build a great ship (around 510 feet long and called an Ark) because He was going to judge the world with this global Flood.

God told Noah that He would send two of every kind (seven of some) of land-dwelling, air-breathing animals to go on board the Ark. Notice that God wasn't saving each and every animal on earth. He saved a set number of each kind of land animal.

In Genesis 6:19-20, we read, *"And of every living thing of all flesh you shall bring two of every sort into the ark, to keep them alive with you; they shall be male and female. Of the birds after their kind, of animals after their kind, and of every creeping thing of the earth after its kind, two of every kind will come to you to keep them alive."*

Noah didn't have to go and find the animals—God brought them to Noah.

Now here is a question for you: Would dinosaurs (and my favorite T-rex) be on board the Ark?

Well, if you read Genesis 6:19-20, you will see that all the land animal kinds were to be on board the Ark. As dinosaurs are included in land animal kinds, then the different kinds of dinosaurs must have been represented on the Ark.

How did the dinosaurs fit on board with other animals; weren't they all too big?

The answer to this is very simple. The average size of a dinosaur skeleton found in the fossil record is only the size of a sheep. We also know that some dinosaurs were as small as chickens! So don't get the idea all dinosaurs were great big monsters.

TIGHT FIT OR ROOM FOR ALL?
Many wonder how Noah could fit all the creatures that God sent to him on the Ark. First, we have to realize the Ark was a large seaworthy craft, like a modern-day oil tanker. It did not look like the child-like bathtub ark that we often see in books and paintings showing animals squeezed in the boat and it threatening to tip over.

By taking representatives of each of the land animal kinds, and not each and every animal that was living at the time, there was plenty of room on this important vessel.

WEATHER OR NOT
As the great Flood begins, there are many questions about what weather conditions might have been at the time. While we cannot answer that question, the Bible provides an important timeline of events related to the Flood in Genesis chapters 7 and 8.

DISAPPEARING DINOSAURS
The great worldwide Flood that occurred during Noah's time answers a lot of questions as to why we find so many dinosaur fossils all over the earth.

PREDATOR OR GREAT PARENT?

The Oviraptor ("egg-robber") is a great example of how dinosaur discoveries can be misinterpreted. This dinosaur was once thought by secular scientists to have robbed the nests of other dinosaurs. This assumption was made because the fossilized bones of an Oviraptor were found very close to a grouping of eggs. After modern technology and other fossil finds showed the eggs were probably those of the Oviraptor found with them, secular scientists then began considering Oviraptors to be caring parents. That conclusion just creates more unproven ideas. One, there is no proof the eggs were deliberately arranged as a nest rather than hurriedly deposited as the mother sought to escape the rising waters of the global Flood. And two, just because the fossil of the adult is found close to the eggs doesn't mean they were actively caring for their offspring. See how information from secular science can seem to be fact but is actually just unproven ideas.

We also know that dinosaurs laid eggs, and the biggest dinosaur egg that has been found is really not that much larger than a football. So even dinosaurs like T-rex and Seismosaurus were very small when they hatched out of eggs.

I suspect that for the fairly large dinosaur that went on the Ark, God would have chosen young adults, that weren't giant in size. Most dinosaurs weren't that big, so they would have no problem fitting on the Ark. So, how could they all fit on the Ark if there were hundreds of kinds of dinosaurs? There might be hundreds of names we give to them, but creation scientists believe there were probably fewer than fifty actual kinds of dinosaurs. The Bible describes animals as belonging to distinct kinds that reproduce more of the same kind. Just like dogs produce more dogs, ceratopsian dinosaurs could produce more ceratopsians.

Let me explain. Today we have many different names for dogs—dingoes, wolves, coyotes, jackals, great danes, poodles, and so on. However, on Noah's Ark there would have been only two dogs that after the Flood became the parents of all the dogs living today. As the dogs moved away from each other over the earth after the Flood, different species of dogs formed, and over time were given different names—but we all recognize them today to be part of just one dog kind.

Now with dinosaurs, there wasn't just one kind—creation scientists think there were probably around 50 kinds. But today, just like with dogs, we give many different names to varieties within a kind. No doubt there was a Brachiosaur kind, a Tyrannosaur kind, a Ceratopsian (including Triceratops) kind, and so on.

The main point I want to make is that there was plenty of room on Noah's Ark for all land animals God sent on board. The Ark only included representatives of each kind.

What happened to all the animals that didn't go on Noah's Ark?

Well, all the land animals not on the Ark would have drowned and then many were buried in mud that has turned into rock, becoming fossils. Most of the dinosaur remains we find as fossils would have come from the Flood of Noah's day. This means these fossils would only be around 4,500 years old! However, many scientists who don't believe the biblical history would say these fossils are millions of years old. But the fossils are not dug up with dates on them, so these scientists just have to theorize, or guess, how old they might be.

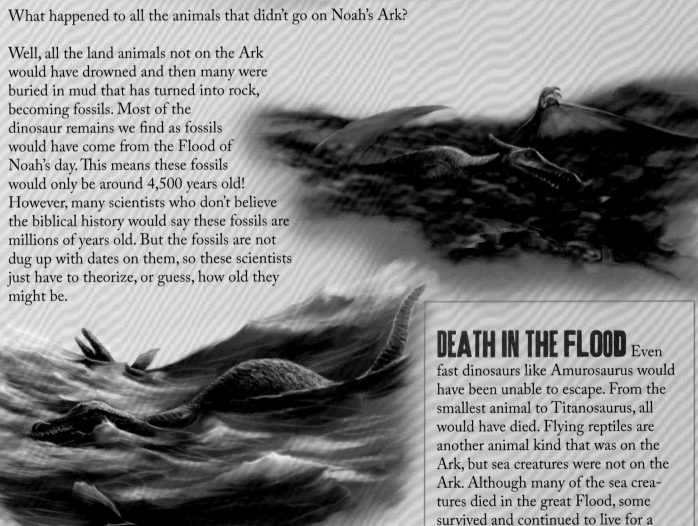

DEATH IN THE FLOOD

Even fast dinosaurs like Amurosaurus would have been unable to escape. From the smallest animal to Titanosaurus, all would have died. Flying reptiles are another animal kind that was on the Ark, but sea creatures were not on the Ark. Although many of the sea creatures died in the great Flood, some survived and continued to live for a time. They eventually became extinct, just like animals become extinct today.

DIFFERENCES WITHIN A KIND

From the very beginning of the Bible, both plants and animals were described as being part of various kinds. The dog kind, camel kind, and the 50 or so dinosaur kinds are just a few examples. Among the various dinosaur kinds you can see a lot of differences, even though they are all still referred to as "dinosaurs."

There can be a lot of variation within the same kind. Ceratopsian ("horned faced") dinosaurs didn't all look the same. These plant-eating dinosaurs included those with one horn, two horns, horns that curved up, horns that curved down, large horn on the nose or a small horn on the nose, smooth skull edges, or bony, spiked edges called frills. In Alberta, Canada, there have already been over a dozen different examples of ceratopsian dinosaurs found—yet they are all part of the same "kind."

Ceratopsians included Albertaceratops, Monoclonius, Arrhinoceratops, Chasmosaurus, Centrosaurus, Avaceratops, Anchiceratops, Brachyceratops, Einiosaurus, Pachyrhinosaurus, Styracosaurus, Nedoceratops, Torosaurus, and many others including the well-known Triceratops.

Look at the differences and similarities between these three examples of the Ceratopsian kind.

WHAT'S EVEN RARER THAN A DINOSAUR FOSSIL?

Dinosaur tracks! Scientists can use these rare finds to try and determine how dinosaurs walked, how fast they could move, and even how much they might have weighed. Some dinosaur track finds can include up to thousands of track prints. An even more unusual dinosaur track was found in Utah. The Copper Ridge Sauropod Track site seems to record an attack in progress (so we know this occurred after sin). Sauropod tracks reveal the creature is turning, and at least four smaller ones are present at the time, as well as what some identify as a large Allosaurus (interpreted as a predator) which made irregular steps that might show that it was injured or limping.

Dinosaur tracks are known as a type of trace fossil—fossils that are not the actual remains of the creature, but a record of some kind of activity it may have done while alive, like making a footprint in the mud that is covered with sand and dirt and preserved. Lark Quarry in Australia holds another unusual example of dinosaur tracks. This site records what seems to be the chaos of a dinosaur stampede.

After the Flood, when the Ark had landed and the ground dried out, God told Noah to open the door and let the animals out into this once beautiful world that was destroyed by the Flood. It was a new beginning.

The animals, including dinosaurs, would have begun reproducing and spreading out over the earth. But it was a much harsher world. It was a much harder place to survive. The great Flood may have destroyed people and animals and even the landscape of the world, but there is one thing it could not destroy. It could not destroy sin. Because sin remained in the world, death was still part of life and people were still separated from God.

THE ARK

The incredible account of Noah's Ark illustrates the concept of salvation. Just as Noah and his family had to go through a door to be saved, so we need to go through a door—the Lord Jesus is our door to salvation. We can say today that Jesus is our Ark of salvation. I trust every one of you reading this book can say, "Yes, I have gone through the door to be saved! I have received this free gift of salvation through Jesus Christ."

AN AMAZING SIGHT!

Imagine being on board Noah's Ark and seeing all the animals living in harmony during the voyage. Predators and prey were able to live and be cared for side by side without incident, with plenty of room and food for everyone. And dinosaurs of every kind were among the passengers for this incredible adventure!

1. The Ark was made of gopher wood, and was 510 ft long.
2. Studies show the Ark could have survived 100-ft waves.
3. Noah's family and the animals spent 371 days in the Ark.
4. The 420-ft *Tessarakonteres* was another huge ancient wooden ship built around the same time.

ORGANIZED AND ORDERLY

As these illustrations show, life aboard Noah's Ark was an orderly one. With special cage enclosures and Noah's family to care for them, the creatures were well-tended in their designated areas. Wondering how Noah kept the animals from eating one another or Noah's family? The animals were on the Ark because God wanted them to be. He sent them specially to Noah. There would have been food on board for the animals, but perhaps God selected less aggressive animals from the kinds that had become meat eaters since the Fall. Perhaps He miraculously kept them from eating one another. Perhaps God commanded the animals not to, and they obeyed so that the animals would survive and be able to repopulate the earth. God is always in control.

AGE 5: FADED

In the "new" world after the Flood, conditions were not as nice as the previous world. An Ice Age came after the Flood because of the warm waters of the Flood and the cool land and ash in the atmosphere from volcanoes. This Ice Age would have dramatically affected how animals lived and their ability to survive, including the dinosaurs.

Since the Flood, other drastic climate changes have occurred. Some areas that were fertile and well-watered have now changed to deserts. Some dry areas became swamps. Lakes and rivers formed in some areas, while mountains and deep valleys scarred the earth in places.

As a result of the effects of sin, the Fall of man, and now the Flood, harsh ecological conditions, dramatic weather changes, diseases, famines, people clearing land, animals eating each other, and many other reasons, many animal kinds (including dinosaurs) would struggle, eventually starting to die out, and finally becoming extinct.

But if dinosaurs did live after the Flood—perhaps for hundreds or even thousands of years (remember, the Flood was only about 4,500 years ago), then is there any evidence they existed after the Flood?

IN DISTRESS The world following the great Flood was chaotic for animals to live in. Geologic events like volcanoes, the Ice Age, and dramatic weather changes were factors in some dinosaurs becoming extinct.

BEHEMOTH »

Actually, I want to share two major evidences that I believe show clearly that dinosaurs lived with people after the Flood, and even into quite modern times—to within the last few hundred years.

The first evidence is found in the Bible, in the Book of Job, chapter 40. It is here we learn clues about an important creature known as behemoth.

Job lived after Noah's Flood. In Job chapter 40, God describes a great beast that lived beside Job. In fact, in verse 19 of this chapter, this beast, (called Behemoth), is described as *"…the first of the ways of God."* This means it was the largest animal God made. Have a guess at the largest animal to live on earth that we know of at the present? It would be one of the sauropod dinosaurs. Could God be describing a dinosaur to Job? I think so. Let's read on from verses 15 to 18:
"Look now at the behemoth, which I made along with you; He eats grass like an ox. See now, his strength is in his hips, And his power is in his stomach muscles. He moves his tail like a cedar; The sinews of his thighs are tightly knit. His bones are like beams of bronze, His ribs like bars of iron."

JOB AND BEHEMOTH
Clues taken from the Bible tell us about a gigantic creature called behemoth. Note that the biblical passages speak of the creature living, eating, resting, drinking—more clues to this animal being alive and being seen by Job. The great leviathan of the deep is also mentioned in Job and the Psalms.

« LEVIATHAN

Everything about this creature is big and strong—just like you'd expect of a description of a sauropod dinosaur. And notice the tail is compared to a cedar tree. We often read of the cedars of Lebanon—great big cedar trees. Such a description fits the tail of a great sauropod like Argentinosaurus.

Now let's learn about the second great evidence that dinosaurs existed with man in the last few thousand years.

If people really lived at the same time as dinosaurs after the Flood, we would expect to find stories about dinosaurs handed down through the ages.

Many of you may have heard that most cultures, such as the Native Americans, Australian Aborigines, and Babylonian cultures, handed down stories from their ancestors that sounded like the account of Noah's Flood in the Bible.

That's because Noah's Flood was a real event, and as people spread out over the earth they took the account of Noah's Flood with them, and over time changed it somewhat—but we can still see the similarities to the biblical account. Of course, the account of the Flood in the Bible is the true one, and God has ensured it hasn't changed.

Another common group of stories we find in cultures around the world today concern dragon legends. Just as Flood legends are based on a true event—the Flood of Noah's day—I believe dragon legends are based on encounters with real animals—animals that were called dragons by our ancestors but today we call many of these creatures dinosaurs.

Many of the ancient dragon paintings, and dragon sculptures do look like what we expect some of the dinosaurs to look like.

In the 1800s, something interesting happened. A discovery was made that marked the beginning of the next age of the dinosaurs, the age of being Found.

SHARING HISTORY

Much of ancient history was shared by storytellers instead of being written down. Countries around the world have their own versions of legends relating to the great Flood, as well as dragon legends that were probably inspired by dinosaurs. However, God's inspired Word has been handed down in written form and God has specially preserved it.

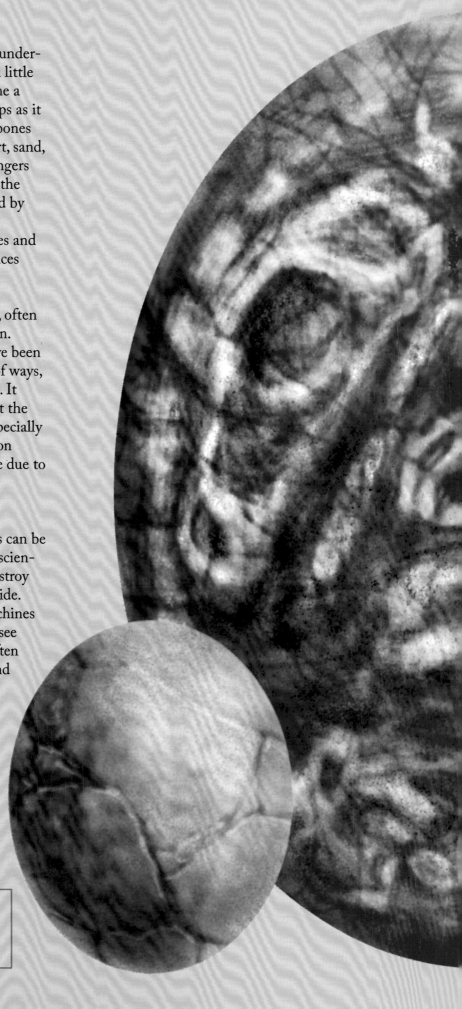

HOW FOSSILS ARE MADE

To understand this discovery, you need to know a little bit about how fossils are formed. Imagine a dinosaur like Baryonyx or a Protoceratops as it died. If all the conditions are right, the bones can become buried by sediments like dirt, sand, or mud, which protect them from scavengers and environmental damage. Sometimes the material making up the bones is replaced by minerals that turn them hard like rock. Sometimes only impressions of the bones and skin are left. There have also been instances where soft tissue has been preserved!

When fossilized remains are discovered, often only broken pieces and fragments remain. Sometimes, we find that many parts have been eroded away, or separated in a number of ways, or jumbled into an unrecognizable mass. It is rare for fossil finds to represent almost the entire skeletal structure of a creature, especially if it was scavenged before the fossilization process began, or broken apart over time due to erosion, earth movements, etc.

EGG-CITING FINDS

Dinosaur eggs can be preserved the same way. Thanks to new scientific advances, scientists don't have to destroy dinosaur eggs in order to see what is inside. Because of the ability of man-made machines to see inside the eggs, just like they can see inside our bodies today, scientists can often identify the type of dinosaur egg it is, and how long the egg had existed before it became fossilized.

Now that you understand how the fossils are preserved, let's explore the next age of dinosaurs. Here these mysterious remains are discovered and scientists try to explain what they were and how these unusual creatures lived and died.

Fossilized dinosaur eggs have been found in China that are 2 feet in length.

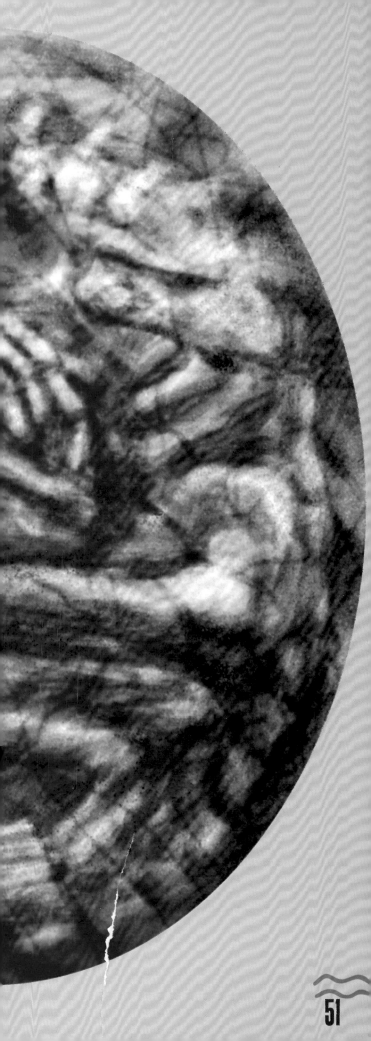

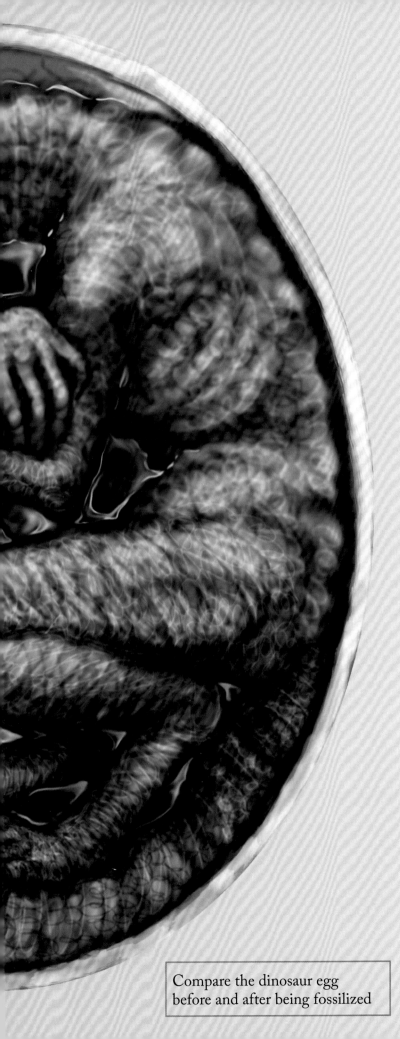

Compare the dinosaur egg before and after being fossilized

WHAT'S INSIDE?

Dinosaur egg fossils are either round or oval in shape. They can differ in terms of texture of the outer shell and thickness of the shell as well as other ways. It is often an incredible challenge to determine the type of dinosaur from the fossilized egg remains.

The first dinosaur eggs ever found were discovered in 1859 in southern France. They were laid by a Hypselosaurus ("highest lizard"), a large sauropod dinosaur over 25 feet long. The Hypselosaurus eggs were a foot in length, and very heavy.

Scientists are slowly beginning to learn more about the structure and details of dinosaur eggs, to help in identifying them. But there is a lot still to be discovered. Mysteries such as how a massive sauropod can be born from a small egg and reach its massive weight and height in its lifetime is just one of them.

Regardless of the many things we don't really know about dinosaurs, we do know that there is no link between dinosaurs and birds (even though both laid eggs), just as there is no link between crocodiles (which lay eggs) and modern-day birds. When trying to solve the mysteries of these mighty dinosaurs, it is important to remember to start with the truth found in the Bible.

FOUR >>>>> FAST FACTS

1. Particle accelerators are now used to create 3-D X-rays of fossils.
2. CT scans are used to show details inside dinosaur eggs or the internal structure of dinosaur skulls.
3. Fossils are fragile so careful excavation and site mapping by hand are used.
4. Resins or chemical coatings are used to strengthen and preserve fossils.

AGE 6: FOUND

Ancient people found the bones of creatures that seemed to belong to a distinct group of land animals no longer alive on earth. Often they thought they represented giants or supernatural creatures from mythology. But in the 1800s, these creatures were "rediscovered" and they began to be studied as real animals that had once lived on the earth.

The first name given to one of these creatures was Megalosaurus. The second to be named was Igaunodon. The man who invented these names was the same scientist who created the word "dinosaur," Sir Richard Owen. He considered them to be part of this dinosauria group. This is probably why many people think all dinosaurs were great monsters. But we all know now that is not true—most dinosaurs were quite small. As I said earlier, the average size being that of a sheep.

Once these creatures were rediscovered, people became fascinated by what they were, how they lived, what they looked like, and how they died. They began to study the fossil remains, and develop ideas or make guesses about the lives of these creatures.

Some of their beliefs seemed at first to make a lot of sense. But sadly, secular scientists began choosing to believe unproven ideas from men rather than the truth of God's Word. Secular scientists study the present age of dinosaurs with a belief in evolution and the false idea that the earth is millions of years old.

TOO COLD OR JUST RIGHT?

Dinosaur fossils can be found throughout the world, including the polar regions. But this doesn't mean that these dinosaurs actually lived there. It is important to remember that before the great Flood when Noah lived, the continents were different than they are now. That means that the bones found in the arctic could have originally been part of a continent that was elsewhere and then rearranged during the great Flood. Or the dinosaur bones could have come from a different place and simply been left in that area by the Flood waters.

WHAT IS FOSSILIZED?

1. Skin patterns reveal scales, armored plates, or special features in addition to texture.

2. Impressions of wings, muscle, bones, and more can reveal body structure.

3. Internal organs can reveal size and possibly the internal organ's structure.

4. Dinosaur droppings called coprolites can show what the dinosaur was eating—but it is impossible to determine exactly what kind of dinosaur it was.

5. Teeth marks can reveal what kind of dinosaur might have killed or scavenged the remains.

6. Some injuries to dinosaurs have left evidence of infection, breaks, healed areas, and more.

7. The shape of bones and skeletal structure, the size and shape of the teeth, and the structure of blood vessels can be observed.

8. Fossil tracks can help us to estimate the speed of dinosaurs.

9. Dinosaur eggs can reveal embryos of dinosaurs before birth.

10. Many fossils reveal insects, plants, fish, flowers, seeds, and even animal burrows.

THE SAGA OF SUE

Displayed in the Chicago Field Museum, "Sue," the largest and most complete T-rex fossil found to date, has had a turbulent history. Years of legal battles and finally a record-breaking auction, led to "Sue" finding a museum home in Chicago.

Disputes over legal ownership of Sue highlighted many of the inconsistencies and voids in the law when it comes to fossil discoveries.

The best fossils are highly prized and are often sold at auction, many to private collectors who don't make them available to be studied or viewed by the public. Many feared that Sue would meet a similar fate when it went up for auction in 1997.

Discovered in 1990 on a Cheyenne reservation near Faith, South Dakota, Sue was a chance find from tiny bones found at the base of a cliff. Over 80 percent complete, the discovery was soon a media sensation.

After studying the bones, scientists think that Sue was around 30 years old at the time of its death. But they don't know if Sue was a male or a female T-rex. Very few T-rex fossils have been found so far.

FOUR >>>>> FAST FACTS

1. Sue is forty feet long from its nose to tail, and twelve feet tall at the hip.
2. The fossil is named for the paleontologist that discovered it.
3. The skull on display is not the original one; a lighter, steel cast without the damage is mounted in its place.
4. Sue isn't the only T-rex with a name. "Jane" is a juvenile T-rex found in 2001.

BONES TELL THE TALE

After being cleaned, parts of Sue's skeleton was scanned by CT machines. This technology allows scientists to see imperfections or damage to the bones, as well as generate 3D models using special software. These are the same machines that are used in diagnosing human diseases, tumors, and other medical conditions in hospitals around the world. Scientists study growth lines in the bones to try to determine how old Sue may have been when it died and how quickly T-rexes may have grown.

MUSEUM DISPLAYS

Could you tell just by looking that Sue's skull was not the real one? It's hard to tell sometimes in museum displays. And often museum displays either show or talk about details that scientists really don't know are fact, but represent their own ideas that they present as the truth. A lot of questions about how dinosaurs lived cannot be answered by the very elaborate displays. When you know this, you won't be confused when you see information that conflicts with the biblical truth about dinosaurs. When you look at these displays with a biblical worldview, then you can begin to work out what is fact and what is fiction.

PRESERVED BY PLASTER

Sue's bones, like many other fossil finds, were persevered by a process of wrapping them first in foil and then in plaster-soaked burlap strips. This is a process known as field jacketing, which has been used for over a hundred years. Later, cast replicas of the bones are made.

PIECES PUT TOGETHER

Workers at the museum began putting the pieces together to create the display of Sue's bones. They positioned the bones to reflect how they think Sue may have stood, and created additional supporting exhibits to tell what secular scientists think Sue's life and death may have been like.

AGE 7: FICTION

When we read a book about make-believe things, we call it a book of fiction. When we read a book about true things, we call it a book of "non-fiction."

This book you are reading is a "non-fiction" book. It is the true history of the world, explaining dinosaurs based on the record of the Creator God in the Bible and careful observation of what is actually found in the present.

However, in this modern age, there are many people who don't want to obey God. They don't want to acknowledge they are sinners in need of salvation. They don't want God telling them what is right and wrong.

Such people need an explanation for how life and the universe came to be—but it is an explanation without God. They teach that life arose billions of years ago just by chance, rather than as part of God's plan. This story is part of the idea called "evolution."

BOOKS OF FICTION

They believe somehow matter, or "goo," or "slime" produced life, and then one kind of creature changed into another kind of creature over millions of years. They believe dinosaurs evolved around 200 million years ago, and then they eventually evolved into birds. Then 65 million years ago dinosaurs supposedly died out for some mysterious reason. Then they believe that around 2 million years ago, ape-like creatures began evolving into humans—and here we are today! Of course, those who believe this were not there in the past and don't know everything—they just believe this had to happen. It is a way to explain life without acknowledging the power and truth of our Creator God.

People who believe in evolution and millions of years have written many books about this topic, including thousands and thousands of books about dinosaurs. But such books, based on evolution, are really books of fiction—they are simply not true.

A BELIEF THAT JUST DOESN'T FLY

A biblical worldview answers many of the questions about where dinosaurs came from, how they lived, and why their fossils are found today. Evolutionists try to answer the same questions, though they put their trust in evolution and the false belief that the earth is millions of years old.

In an to attempt to prove Charles Darwin's idea of evolution, scientists have long sought what they call transitional fossils. These are fossils that they believe will supposedly show a link between two unrelated fossils—proving that one creature evolved into another. A transitional fossil linking dinosaurs and birds for example, has been sought for over 100 years.

Though discovered in Germany in 1860, it was not until the 1970s that the fossil of Archaeopteryx became what many considered to be the "missing link" between birds and dinosaurs. Thought to be more dinosaur than bird, it and a few other fossil discoveries in China were believed to support the idea that dinosaurs evolved into birds. But Archaeopteryx is now simply considered a bird, not the transitional fossil many thought it was. It was shown from an evolutionist perspective to be older than the dinosaur fossils it supposedly evolved from. And other fossils that once appeared to have "feathers" have turned out to be woven skin fibers instead.

Could a dinosaur have feathers? God created many animals that have similar features, but they are still distinctly different animals. Because of differences—blood, lungs, hip structure, and more—it makes no sense scientifically to say modern birds evolved from dinosaurs. And to date, no feathered dinosaurs have been found or any other fossil that proves this idea.

Birds and flying reptiles like pterosaurs were created on Day 5, while dinosaurs were created separately on Day 6 with other land animals.

FOLLOW THE TRUTH While the Bible helps us to understand how and when dinosaurs lived, and even why they died, the Bible doesn't give us highly descriptive details about each and every one. It gives us the big picture of history so we can develop a general understanding of these creatures. Then we can use observational science to help us fill in some of the details and increase our understanding—all the while knowing that nothing in real science can or will contradict God's Holy Word.

Based on how animals live today, we believe that some dinosaurs lived in great herds like cattle, while others lived solitary lives or in small family groups. We know what some of them looked like in terms of the texture of their skin, though not the colors they may have displayed, and we can even guess how they may have reacted to certain situations. We can only guess on how they may have communicated, though science has managed to recreate the sounds a few dinosaurs may have made based on bone and other skeletal features.

What scientists cannot absolutely prove as a fact is simply a guess, or in some cases when it does not follow the truth of God's Word, it is fiction.

FOUR >>>> FAST FACTS

1. In ancient China, fossils were thought to be the remains of dragons.
2. Ancient Greeks believed that fossil bone beds were where giants had fought.
3. Even in modern China, some dinosaur fossils are ground into a powder and sold as medicine.
4. Numerous ancient cities and areas were named because of the fossil finds discovered there.

And that brings us to the most important part of this book. This is a non-fiction book about dinosaurs, written at a time when there is so much fictional information about dinosaurs.

Some important questions about dinosaurs have been answered with the help of the Bible. The seven biblical "Fs," the seven ages of dinosaur history, are very important to understand because of all the misinformation about dinosaurs that is so common today.

The Bible is the most important book in the entire universe, a book that is totally accurate in every way, with no mistakes—the only book of its kind. It tells us who God is. It tells us about the history of our world, the history of dinosaurs, and the history of people. It tells us how to live, and what God expects from us.

The Bible is not only the true history book of the universe, but it is the only book that really tells where we came from (that God created the first man and woman from whom we have descended), what our problem is (that we are sinners and thus separated from God), and what the solution to our problem is (to receive the free gift of salvation—to go through the one who says He is the door, the Lord Jesus, who is the door to our Ark of salvation).

If you have never gone through that door and received Jesus as your Ark of salvation, why don't you do that now by praying the following prayer:

Dear God,
Thank You for creating the world and all the animals like dinosaurs. Thank You for creating me and loving me even though I am a sinner. I believe You sent your Son, Jesus, to die for me and my sins. I don't want to be separated from You by sin any more. I repent of my sin. I love You and receive Jesus Christ as my Savior. I want to be obedient to Your will for my life and my future. Amen.